San Antonio Review

Winter 2019 | Issue Two

© Copyright 2019. San Antonio Review. All rights reserved.

The moral rights of the authors have been asserted.

Cover design by Misty Cripps. All rights reserved.
Interior design by William O. Pate II.

Print ISBN: 978-1-0878-0092-9 | Ebook ISBN: 978-1-0878-0093-6
KDP ISBN: 9781693640360 | Also available on Kindle and other eBooks.

The *San Antonio Review* is San Antonio's international literary journal.

The *San Antonio Review* is brought to you by

William O. Pate II, Editor & Publisher
william@sa-review.com

Alex Z. Salinas, Poetry Editor
alex@sa-review.com

Gianna Sannipoli, Reader & Reviewer
gianna@sa-review.com

Misty Cripps, Designer
mistycripps@gmail.com

Brianna Keeper, Artist-in-Residence (Painting)
briankeeper@gmail.com

www.sa-review.com

POETRY EDITOR'S NOTE | ALEX Z. SALINAS 6
NOTE FROM THE EDITOR & PUBLISHER | WILLIAM O. PATE II 8

POETRY 10

UPON RAILS OF DISTRACTION | DIANE GONZALES BERTRAND 11
QUE NO PUEDO ENTREGAR | BRITTANY LEITNER 12
THE TRUTH ABOUT BUBBLES | CHARLIE BRICE 13
THERE ARE TIMES OF SILENCE | ACE BOGGESS 14
PUMPING GAS | JESSE BREITE 15
GET ON YOUR KNEES | LUIS CUAUHTÉMOC BERRIOZÁBAL 16
OIL OR MEN | DAVID TAYLOR 17
OVER A FAR CITY A RAINBOW | EMMA LEE 18
THE GREAT THING ABOUT BEING SOMETIMES HISPANIC | ALEX Z. SALINAS ... 19
SHARK SOUP | ALEX Z. SALINAS 20
ALL THE NAMELESS SAINTS | JOHN SWEET 22
KID BROTHER DROPOUT | KEVIN RIDGEWAY 24
LARRY SMITH: AN APPRECIATION | MIKE JAMES 25
ELVIS RESURRECTION | LARRY SMITH 28
WOMEN'S HAIR | LARRY SMITH 30

PHOTOGRAPHY 31

NEON CENTURY | MICHELLE BROOKS 32
UNITED WE STAND | MICHELLE BROOKS 33
CANDY CANE, BUFFETS CANDY SHOP | MICHELLE BROOKS 34

FICTION 35

GOWN MEN AND THE SIREN | JOHN BONANNI 36
THE PHOTO IN YOUR COAT POCKET | B.J. FISCHER 41
MEN WITHOUT HEARTS, INC. | ALEX Z. SALINAS 47

ESSAYS 52

A SCHOOL BOARD MEETING CHALLENGES FAITH | BEKAH S. MCNEEL 53
VIRGINITY | JERI GRIFFITH 57

PAINTINGS 61

LIBERALS | BRIANNA KEEPER 62
BIG LAFAYETTE | BRIANNA KEEPER 63
FIREHOLE CANYON | BRIANNA KEEPER 64

MORE POETRY 65

DON'T WAKE ME UP, JUST YET | MIKE JAMES 66
OCD | JOSHUA LINDENBAUM 67
SANCTUARY | JAMES H. DUNCAN 68
SISTER CITIES | ABBY MANGEL 69
JUNE 25TH | RUDY MARTINEZ 70
A CYNIC IS A MAN | DAVID MATTHEWS 72

Feeding the Fish | Rebecca Schumejda 73
Sunny Lake Crazy | Rex Wilder 74
White with a Little Shade | Joel Fry 75
A Teacher's Hope: Being Remembered | David A. Grenardo 76
Neptune's Son | Daniel Edward Moore 77
Bending Time | Jennifer R. Lloyd 78

ALL GOOD THINGS 80
Read | Listen | Watch 81
Quotes 82
Contributors 83
Supporters | Thank you! 88

Poetry Editor's Note | Alex Z. Salinas

I want to begin this letter by saying the *San Antonio Review* wasn't my vision, still isn't; all credit goes to Will Pate, *SAR* founder and publisher, for believing in arts and letters within the city of San Antonio and beyond. For launching a grassroots publication out of his own wallet and free time, and then possessing the patience necessary to allow a seed to grow.

Is the *SAR* a tree yet? By no means, in my humble opinion. But perhaps we're now in Baby Groot territory—lovable, sturdy, and here to stay, because our purpose and mission have remained to plant serious roots.

Because of Will's kindness and generosity, I knew after our initial interactions that he and I would stay in contact. However, I never foresaw that he would one day ask me, via text message, "Hey, wanna be poetry editor?" Just like that. That's my guy Will. I had to take him up on the opportunity, even though the work was *pro bono*.

Which leads me to this next sentiment: I'd like to claim that the *SAR* is a passion product—a labor of love—but as I chewed on the latter expression earlier this morning as of this writing, I decided that serious writing, in any form—be it poetry, fiction, essay or memoir—isn't exactly, to my understanding, a labor of love; it's plain hard work. It's grueling, soul-crushing, can pester you day and night and rob you of necessary healing sleep, all because of letters, words, language. This thing called writing, it's difficult to teach, and perhaps even tougher to perform it well. Any writer will attest that there's little that matches the personal satisfaction, the high, of crafting a good sentence.

In the words of my writing mentor and now my friend, Professor Ito Romo, who I can't thank enough for opening my eyes, and my heart, to creative writing in 2015 when I was 26 years old, "Writing is craft." And we writers are obliged to our craft because it's what we love, and also sometimes what we hate.

Good writing, that elusive phoenix, is always our end-goal, the light in the tunnel or the sky that we let lead us through the jungle, the haze and deluge of pain and suffering. Some of us have never emerged from the shadows, have left us work fueled only by darkness.

My hope is that good writing, even at its bleakest, informs us what it is to live well, allow us to make an impression of the short time we have on this earth.

OK, that's enough of my waxing poetic.

I'm happy—overjoyed at times—to be part of the *SAR*, glad to have answered the call when it arrived. I'm happy to have met you wonderful writers whose work appears in these pages and also on our website, happy to have served you to the best of my abilities as well as this craft we've all found ourselves indebted to.

What can I say? Thank you for your support to the *SAR*, to our cause. More importantly, thank you for your continual dedication to good writing, to morphing those foggy, nebulous ideas in your head into something tangible, real; that's craft, the lifeblood that flows through each and every one of us, that through which we live for, and survive.

Alex Z. Salinas
September 2019

Note from the Editor & Publisher |
William O. Pate II

It seems I'll do *almost* anything to avoid my own writing. That what you hold in your hands exists rather than a thick stack of pages of my own scribbles is likely the most physical of evidence of that avoidance. Indeed, the *San Antonio Review* was born of boredom and, in retrospect, a naive self-confidence that continues to financially, mentally and temporally drain me. It nonetheless proves that even persistence in avoiding one's craft can profit it, I hope.

Thus, it is with my pleasure – and not a little surprise – that I present to you the second print issue of the *San Antonio Review*.

My utmost thanks to Alex, Gianna, all our contributors and supporters.

Without Alex, the *San Antonio Review* likely wouldn't still exist. Had he not submitted – both verse to be published, at first, and, later, to my will that he serve as our first poetry editor, thus taking some of the responsibility for reading and *judging* the (also naively) unexpected onslaught of poetry submissions to the *Review* – it's likely, to encroach on Mr. Salinas' own pastoral metaphors, to have died on the vine, as they say. Alex's interest in the *Review*, along with his success in urging others to contribute, has invaluably aided the growth of the *San Antonio Review*.

If I'm honest and tell you that one of my biggest failings is likely loyalty, you'll better understand why, ultimately, I continue to publish the *San Antonio Review* when I say it's mostly out of respect for the work Alex and others have entrusted to us for publication.

Gianna, thank you for the out-of-the-blue offer to help. And thank you for *actually* helping! We expect great things of you, as our new Eastern Europe correspondent. While her influence has so far only been felt in the pieces selected for publication, readers should watch for her work in the *Review*'s future pages.

My thanks especially to Misty, for all the hours she sits across from me at a coffee shop while I stare into a laptop reading submissions, offering writers edits, fiddling with HTML (damn you, WordPress!), designing T-shirts and otherwise maintaining the *Review*.

My most sincere thanks to those of you who have financially contributed to the *San Antonio Review*. I never expect to make any profit on this endeavor. I'm not wealthy, as my ~~selfishly included~~ (I deleted it just before going to publication to save in printing costs) essay on student debt on inadequate.net should clearly illustrate. My income is below the national median. But I tend to think investing in new artists to be worth the cost to our small savings. Thank you for agreeing with me.

Writers, thank you for your submissions. Keep them coming. We can't do this without you – no matter how much I may internally complain about the tedium of, once again, filling up our editorial calendar with new pieces. As the following pages show, we receive stellar submissions. My sincere apologies for your waits for responses.

Finally, thank you, reader, for continuing to read.

William O. Pate II
September 2019

POETRY

Upon Rails of Distraction |
Diane Gonzales Bertrand

I.
Setting sun filters through the streets.
Drivers distracted by tasks, lists,
errands, schedules. Impatient to reach
a destination, sluggish to notice anything
but traffic outside the windshield. Until

the railroad cross bars lower and divide,
red warning signs flash, train whistles echo.
One by one, each car forced to pause, stop, wait.
Disappointment chugs through as the train
rattles over unbending iron tracks, dragging
a line of slow-moving metal companions.

II.
Before modern days of checking cell phones,
Moms used to place the car in park,
turn around and speak to their children, warning
to be on best behavior at Abuelita's house.

Fathers pressed steady on the brakes, admired
different colors, counted styles of train cars,
then spontaneously broke into song,
I've been working on the railroad . . .

III.
Inside our truck, you sigh, shift
into Park. I turn off the radio,
pull a Poem from my purse,
and announce a practice performance.

Each narrative stanza fades away
as dusk arrives. The last line ends
just as the wooden cross bars rise up.

Drivers rouse from their diversions,
moving like trains upon rails of distractions.

Que No Puedo Entregar |
Brittany Leitner

after i finally write about being
mexican i am told i can't write
a whole book about being mexican

i tell my boyfriend he is white
privilege and he smiles because
i have it too i

don't know what i have when no
one is looking but i think of my
mom and she is the mexican one

i know *el chico del apartamento cinco
doce* but it's not because my mom
told me about him it's my sister she

sings to him near the stereo
and i wonder if he sits on the
stoop like me and has big plans

to tell the world he's not
mexican or if he'll always be trapped
in that song *que no puedo entregar* i

sit and try to untangle my
blood but my veins snap like
accordion pulls and they come

back to form the *mariachi* band
that lives on my shoulder and
sings to me when i cannot dream

The Truth about Bubbles |
Charlie Brice

For her work on bubbles Karen Uhlenbeck
became the first woman to win
the Abel Prize in mathematics which
now should be renamed the Eve Prize.

From those effervescent multi-colored bumps
in after-dinner sinks, to those ethereal
transparent balls blown into space by childish
lips, to the huge black hole (a big bubble
born of a dying star) in the Messer 87 galaxy,
55 light years from earth, beautifully
photographed in today's *New York Times*,
bubbles permeate everything.

Who doesn't enjoy bubbles—blameless
pockets of plash even when produced
by lava flow or tsunami? They're only
along for the ride. They mean no harm.

Perhaps all of us live in a bubble—a hidden
iridescent dome of good intentions and
bon amis. If Professor Uhlenbeck would only
discover its area, compute its circumference,
realize its radius, we'd dance on thermals
of brotherhood and goodwill until, like a sparkle
of soap suds, we'd burst into the ether,
neverlasting, like a star.

There Are Times of Silence |
Ace Boggess

when my head whirs & clatters like a dusty fan.
I can't close the browser window in my brain
long enough to enjoy a blank screen,
ease into an afternoon of rest.

I should be doing X, I think. *She said Y, but why?* I think.
*The government is, the country is, the ignorance of men,
my own. I'm a failure & a god*, I think,
ideas passing in contrails rather than lasting comets' tails.

Talk to myself, although it's not me to whom I speak,
but those I know: my head full of full conversations
we won't have in dim bars or crowded halls
innocuously passing. Sometimes songs erupt inside:

dormant volcanos believed extinct. I don't wish
to sing along, so listen as if to a stereo through the wall.
I can't mute it, can't make out words I once memorized
in ghost-gray off-key melodies like these.

Pumping Gas | Jesse Breite

A man walks from pump to
pump asking for … you know
what he's asking for, and I
don't want to see his face.
I don't want to be convinced
by some jugular detail.
Behind the SUV door, I've
already made up my mind
he's not worthy for—what it always
comes back to—my resources.
Men have died for the slick
I pour into the back of my car.
Besides, I've filled his tank before.
I've bought his dinner, paid
more than I ought for Girl Scout Cookies.
When I clutch my wallet to swipe,
I want to pull out my diaper bill,
show what I pay for water alone!
Last time I bought some homeless
dude's dinner, his cell went off
while he ordered the biggest meal
on the menu, and I didn't say it
but I wanted to ask why he couldn't
just phone a friend for his Baconator.
I squeeze the pump in my hand.
Here he comes—and dammit,
I prepare my best *take a hike/*
you don't know the troubles I've seen bit.
He reaches in the trash to grab
an open bag of Fritos, stares through me
for no satisfaction, and takes himself
mumbling down the sidewalk.

Get on Your Knees |
Luis Cuauhtémoc Berriozábal

In hell the beer is
never cold enough,
the music is not
loud enough, and a
kiss gives you herpes.

What did you expect,
the royal treatment?
Get on your knees and
crawl through the sharpest
glass, the hottest coal,

and remember what
you did to get here.
Enjoy your beer on
earth, turn up the rock
n' roll. It will not

get better than this.
Kiss the one you love
and mean it. The sharp
glass and hot coals are
being made for you.

Oil or Men | David Taylor

The first white girl I had sex with
never accused me of rape,
though her father did.

Why else would his daughter
spread her legs for a black man.

One day he showed her
how to check the oil in her car
and slapped her mouth so hard
she cracked a right front tooth.

He said she never listened,
about oil or men—
and that she'd fuck any black boy
that gave her the time of day.

Her mother tried to cover it all up,
popped more pills to pretend
his fist was an empty palm,
that his knuckles were the rosary.

That night I said we could live somewhere
he didn't have a map to,
but she told me I should leave instead.

Even today, I still want to kill him
for the pain that grew inside her,
even though I can no longer remember
what she looked like walking away.

Over a Far City a Rainbow |
Emma Lee

A queen bee switched her daughter's diet
to honey and pollen, withholding the royal jelly.
She feared her hive had a second queen.

The queen's five eyes scoured her daughter's cell,
kept it light so nothing was hidden. The larva
was punished for any signs of independence.

An untended larvae will shrivel. Forced
to become a worker, she gave the queen
pre-digested news and praise but felt sick.

The queen buzzed rage at her daughter's failures,
took credit for successes. The daughter owned
nothing. She dieted in preparation to fly.

In a far city, the daughter found a room
with a bed, a bookcase, a cupboard and desk.
Band posters darkened the room's walls.

Record boxes and books over-spilled the shelves.
The daughter focused her listening to songs
she could dream dance routines for.

A rainbow messaged: there are flowers here.
In moonlight, the daughter grew and tested her wings.
She didn't have to be the queen to live.

The Great Thing About Being Sometimes Hispanic |
Alex Z. Salinas

The part when I infiltrate the imperialist hive,
But not the part when my wings fall off

The part when I afford to shop at Target,
But not the part when I still eat Taco Bell

The part when my skin looks white,
But not the part when it tans after a hike

The part when I speak un poquito Spanish,
But not the part when I can't communicate with Grandma

The part when I earn a college degree,
But not the part when I can barely pay for it

The part when I have many brothers and sisters,
But not the part when there're three mothers

The part when my father pronounces "chair" *sher*,
But not the part when we laugh at him

The part when I am mistaken for full white,
But not the part when my name sounds full brown

The part when I am blessed with rhythm,
But not the part when I hate to dance

The part when I got it goin' on in my pants,
But not the part when I can't keep it in

The part when I dreamt I was white,
But not the part when I opened my eyes

The part when I dream I am Hispanic,
But not the part when I open my eyes

Shark Soup | Alex Z. Salinas

I have an irrational fear in the shower
when I close my eyes
that a shark will burst through the tile wall
and devour me whole

Perhaps that's because within the red waters
in the chambers of my heart,
there lurks a shark
with an appetite unceasing
till it has swallowed every top floater alive

My heart is encased in shark teeth,
is a rubber shield of death impenetrable

Except to you,
who pried it open when your lips
locked on mine and your tongue
searched for sustenance
like a hungry shark

My irrational fear is you

Our first kiss
every time
reminds me
every time
of your delicious core,
which beats like a revolutionary fist,
gushes like punctured skin from a mortal wound

And like a good vampire shark,
I open my serrated jaws,
sink my razor teeth in you,
deep in you, my love,
past your cream dermis walls

till I find
that which is all alone,

unprotected

Then I feed from it.

all the nameless saints |
John Sweet

de chirico's shadows, late afternoon,
end of winter with sunlight as
weak as christ

gotta laugh when the
fist finds the child's throat

gotta be some lesser god shooting
stray dogs
down by the river

it's easy

not enough time in the day to
start worrying about the future

your father dies and then
your brother but
the bills still have to be paid

girlfriend keeps crying every
time you fuck her sister and
this is how the days pass

minutes scrape and hours bleed

a lifetime spent crawling through
sewers thick with disease is
more than some of us deserve
but you'd be a fool to think
you have a choice

you'd be a liar if you said that
begging for the pain

didn't make you happy

or maybe it's myself
i'm talking about here

Kid Brother Dropout |
Kevin Ridgeway

I wanted to be just like my older brother;
tired of being known as just Sean's kid brother,
so I wanted to be his equal or surpass him.
I auditioned for the same role he won awards
for my senior year but I lost the role to a friend.
And I was passed over by my brother's college,
an inferior little man in the shadows of the great one
I must bow to but instead I rebelled and became
a bearded freak in the green mountains of Vermont,
doing drugs and fueling my damaged little ego
with a new frontier of possibilities big brother
could never dream of after a slight bit
of chemical brain damage freed me of the need
to compare myself to him or want to kick him
in the eye with my cowboy boots wrestling him
on the living room carpet back in 1984
when I fought dirty and tried to bite his dick off,
still fighting dirty to this day in order to overcome
my lack of an identity after years of not knowing
who to be as the youngest in a family
of worldwide superstars.

Larry Smith: An Appreciation |
Mike James

Some writers we discover bit by bit. We put them in one category — novelist, poet, journalist, critic, biographer — and often ignore their work as an entirety. It's easy to do that, and understandable. Writers who are accomplished in multiple genres make a short list. Larry Smith belongs on that list.

The first book I read by Smith was his very fine biographical study of the poet and publisher Lawrence Ferlinghetti. It's tempting to see Ferlinghetti as a role model for Smith. Both are poets who established presses (Ferlinghetti's City Lights and Smith's Bottom Dog.) Both are highly educated, but write in a vernacular, streetwise, American English. Both love travel, the underdog and the unexpected epiphany. And both are hard-headed, often wrong-headed and tough in a very eccentric American way.

Smith's book on Ferlinghetti displays his talents as a critic, but it is Smith's biography of Kenneth Patchen which displays a lifetime's passionate reading and study. *Kenneth Patchen: Rebel Poet in America* should be required reading for every writing program in the country. Through tremendous research and an empathy born from the same Ohio working-class roots which birthed Patchen, Smith takes the reader on a journey through the poet's pain-racked, but productive life.

Through his scholarship and his work at Bottom Dog Press, Smith has done more than almost anyone else to keep Patchen's work in the literary landscape. Bottom Dog has published books of Patchen's poetry, books on his art and books of his correspondence. Smith has been tireless in his devotion to and support of Patchen.

Unlike Patchen, most of Smith's poetry is grounded in the everyday. He is comfortable in the woods and in cheap diners. He looks at textile plants and streetlights. It's common to find the characters in Smith's poems, "living in the house of a friend / wearing his old clothes as my own." Most of Smith's people are ones who are "avoiding poverty by wanting less."

Smith's poetry is grounded in his study of Zen. He's made some vivid translations from the Japanese poet Ryokan which show a strong affinity in temperament and subject matter. "Long Winter Night" is one of those typically good translations (done with Mei Hui Liu Huang):

> In old age memories of a boyhood return:
> myself along reading in a huge hall.
> I've replaced oil in my lamp often tonight.
> Back then, I couldn't tell the length of night.

It would be a mistake to think Smith is a poet who only knows the local and whose imagination never carries him further than a Zen acceptance of suffering and never flies beyond the skyline of the next town. Smith can seem a poet whose imagination frolics in the surreal. Take "Deliveries" from his early collection *Echo Without Sound*:

> A lunchbox suddenly dreams it's a hotel
> with rooms, restaurants, and a heated pool.
> It dreams itself awake.
> No one will touch it now. It's not what they expect.
> They wanted more. They wanted less.

What I love about the poem is the way it takes the reader to a completely different place. It's surreal and it's odd and even though it doesn't make logical sense, it still makes me smile because my mind is in a different location after just five lines.

His most recent book, *The Pears*, has the same comfort with the imagination, but the narrator is sager. "The Writing" shows what he can do:

> Don't go running off to
> pick out a cut tree

then bring it into the house
and load it with gaudy decorations.

Dig a small one from the earth at night
and drag it along the ground,
then pot and place it on the porch
leaves and bugs and all
where rain and snow can feed it.

His new book combines his knowledge of the everyday with an imagination that takes chances. He inhabits a place where, "our coats become our lovers / our gloves are dark tattoos."

Elvis Resurrection | Larry Smith

By the time they pack us up again, I'm ready to move. Five years boxed, standing up in an old warehouse—it's about time. Hey, how is that to treat a king! King of Rock that is—"Elvis in the warehouse," the other dummies joke. But I always knew that one day I'd be back on top, showman that I am, featuring at some classy New York museum or Vegas casino. Word is, a bunch of us from Niagara's old "Celebrities in Wax House" are being moved to the Midwest. Not my choice, but, hey, Elvis is big everywhere. We stars, Liz and Liza, Bogie and Bacall, Kennedy and Nixon, and a bunch of others are all being loaded up. We'll need a supporting cast.

The train ride is pretty dull, but that's normal for us who stand and wait outside any concept of time. Like horses and cattle, we sleep standing up. If they lay us down, see, we begin to sag and warp. You don't want that and neither do I. Believe me.

At the station in Cleveland we're loaded onto a freight truck. I can see through the cracks and hear the workers cursing the lifting. Little do they know whom they handle—the famous transported in the back of a truck. Pretty ironic. But I do understand such security measures. People always want to touch me or worse, and there was that awful woman in Niagara.

When the truck finally stops, the doors slide up. The light hits us, and all I can see is a big red brick building with the words "Silver Lining Cathedral" in big white letters. My name's not yet reached the marquee or billboards. The workers unload us onto dollies, and suddenly another group of buildings appear, probably our trailers near the set.

Once inside, we are stripped down, our show garments exchanged for costumes, my gold lamé folded on a chair. Naked in wax, nothing really moves or matters. Let them look. I was made to show it all, with all my anatomy clearly intact. The costume women look up and giggle as they unwrap a long cloth, a robe it seems . . . for the King. But why such humble cloth? It seems ancient and common, yet, as they say, "Anything for the film." At first, a hood comes over my head, then wisely someone allows my face to be seen. "Never hide your star."

I'm being carried into a room with three walls, our set no doubt. Others are standing robed before me assembled in waiting before a gray-blue sky with a lightning streak. There's Natalie over there kneeling with Jennifer by the rocks. Edward G. and Vincent are holding long, pointed spears. I'm waiting for my blocking when the director calls out something, and my robe is taken off, my arms are being raised and carefully reattached. I am the figure to be placed — up there in the light. My God! Oh, my God. It's the cross!

As wounds are being painted on my legs and hands, I think of Mother, and a beautiful smile comes over my face. I feel it—we are, all us, in a Bible wax museum.

Women's Hair | Larry Smith

smoke rising from a campfire
deep scent of the seasons
sugar sprinkled on bread and butter
fingers interlacing hands
threads woven into a scarf of
black and red, brown and yellow
silk against the face
french curves inside themselves
dangling at the breasts
a crest of tender nakedness
touch the soul, kiss the sky
sweet Marys in a glass of wine

PHOTOGRAPHY

Neon Century | Michelle Brooks

Albuquerque, New Mexico
Nikon
August 2018

United We Stand | Michelle Brooks

Ferris, Texas
Nikon
June 2019

Candy Cane, Buffets Candy Shop |
Michelle Brooks

Albuquerque, New Mexico
Nikon
January 2019

FICTION

Gown Men and the Siren |
John Bonanni

Belief creates tradition, and when left to man, becomes superstition.

And superstition is the seed of prejudice.

Jefferson Parish, 1940
The hole in the ceiling of the camelback house shown a ray of light through the empty backroom. The house filled with laughter and fresh fried catfish on Butler Street when Beatrice called her family to dinner. They lived, separate and unequal, within this world run by Gown Men and the Siren.

That's the way it was. No one complained.

Except the sweeper boy, Beatrice's youngest son. Lloyd would hide away in the tin-roofed shed and dream. The hole in the ceiling was a way of knowing things, and when he moved the can away that collected rain on stormy days, he could tell how angry the Siren was by the number of drops that fell into the can. He could tell the mood of the world from that hole.

On sunny days, he could see planes taking off at the nearby airport. He wondered where those planes went, and he knew he would have to find out. He watched his father dig trenches for septic pipes, and he didn't want that for himself. Even though his father dug the septic pipes all over town, he did not want that. He even dug for the high school across the street. But the sweeper boy never attended that school. He was not allowed by the Gown Men. If you stayed in your 'hood west of the Esplanade in *Tremè* or just across the street in Kenner, you had no trouble. You just had to stay in your place. There was no other way. Sheriff made sure of that.

A Bartender serving up Sazerac, a specialty of the house, 1950
I work at Commander's Palace. I work the bar, but not at lunch, only dinner. Too many sightseers looking for the new 25-cent martini at lunch. You know they are outsiders because they talk silly about

nothing. They may well be foreigners. And I like to stay out of my neighbor's trouble. Like one of them talked like he knew all about the levee and the floods. He spoke no truth. He is a visitor and he will be gone soon.

I told him about that house on Butler Street. I'd say the rampart by Butler in Jefferson Parish was about 15 feet taller than that last house on the road. The house was really a lean-to, a shack; weathered, gray slats of pine clinging to rotting posts sunken in sandy loam. Once, the shack was almost flattened on the Siren's last visit. The wind pulled and pushed so strong it looked like the shack tried to up and leave the wrath of rain and wind on its own, as if it stretched itself to pull away from its foundations and make a run for it. I saw this myself. It stood the ground, though. Figured it was out to remind people: *Remember what happened here*. The shack stayed its roots. It had its own life.

Once, it was sturdy, standing bright white over mossy greens made moist by swamp water seeping from the levee. You could shore up the levee all day long and the Siren would inevitably make her way, pushing and pushing against the giant berm of earth; always threatening to overcome like an unholy goddess with revenge in her heart. She lived in that water just beyond the levee, ready to take you and thrash you about, like a soaked ragdoll. She'd whip you round and round faster and faster, watching the spray of wetness leave you. Then, when you'd dried out and come to, she'd rear back as far as she pleased and hurl you into the cold green-black soup of the Miss'ippi. A Siren, she was. Every inch of her beauty paid for by those who dared to turn back and challenge her titillating fury.

We are Napoleonic Code here in Jefferson Parish. We don't trouble our neighbor and our neighbor don't trouble us. Except when they do. Then, the Gown Men take care of things. You may think you are in America, but you are Napoleonic Code here. It's different here. Was French. Was Spanish. So, America come last. You can have your *muffuletta* and your *beignets* and your drink in *Vieux Carre*, but you must eventually leave, because if you don't, either the Siren or the Gown Men will get you.

Then there are the masks. There are specific reasons for the masks. They protect us. That's why the Gown Men wear them.

Come Mardi Gras, you know a foreigner when you see them make fools of themselves putting the masks on, dancin' like thoughtless clowns and mimicking them, singin' and dancin' with them. But when they do that, they dishonor the power of those masks. They mock them. And then, the foolish clowns are gone. For as sure as I am standing here wiping the bar, you will be gone too, if you mock the mask.

Once, at the Lundi Gras, the night of the arrival of King Rex and King Zulu, I seen a boy mock a Master Masquerader's mask. He danced around him real close sayin', "I don't need no mask, my face already colored." Then the sheriff come. He came between the boy and the Master Masquerader. He told the boy to go home. I guess he did.

I not seen that boy since over a year now. Missed school and all. Didn't show up for work at the icehouse. Probably got lazy again and stayin' in neighborhood by the Esplanade, away from trouble. I hope, anyway. But we don't speak of who is not there anymore.

Here, the Siren rules the water and the wind, and the Gown Men rule the land and fire. They knew the law and the power, and if they needed to, they show it with fire, bright white like the lean-to in Kenner, bright white, like an outside church.

When the Gown Men set a place for gathering up, Sheriff let them run their business there, since nobody wanted that house on Butler Street anymore, being right by the levee and abandoned and all. No one went there. Nobody wanted to be in between the Gown Men and the Siren of the levee. The water of the Siren or the fire of the Gown Men, it *don' madda*.

There was righteousness there. When there was trouble, a night at the shack by the levee set things straight. I seen trucks there, trucks I know that people owned, but I didn't see them. I seen figures, in masks, in gowns, like spirits. Just like the Siren. *Soc au lait!* You heard her howl, you felt the whip of her wind, the slap of her watery waves, but you never saw her. But you knew she was there. And when the Gown Men did their outside church, cross and all, it was a sight to behold. The riverboat crews knew the Gown Men was at church service when they would see the bright white light on the horizon below, like a boiling cauldron cleansing the stains of wrongdoing and making it white again. When it was finished, it was right again. *Laissez les bons temps rouler.* Let the good times roll.

New Orleans, 1953

Downtown on Canal and Rampart, Dave Bartholomew, an established R&B conductor, picked up a baton and directed a young pianist named Fats to play for the first recording artist scheduled for the day.

The artist sang a ditty he had played back when he was a sweeper boy at a defunct restaurant by the airport. The young man, without sheet music or training, became a musician that day. He remembered his *Nainain*, his godmother, who had cured his headache the night before by taking his head in her hands and invoking the name of *Agwe*, the goddess of the sea and marine life. His headache left him after the incantation.

The Bartender, wiping the bar for the last customer, 1960

I don't know about no Mambo or Lychee. That's the practice of the Esplanade folks. They keep their distance, they keep their peace, and I don't need to know them or their habits. *Beaucoup crasseux*, I hear. Very dirty. They are wild and sometimes can wake the Siren up. Then they get whipped and thrashed about, and the Siren pours her wrath over the levee and takes some of them out to sea with her.

When the Siren is pleased, everyone celebrates, even the *Boogalee* with *Fais do do*, with maybe a few less. But no one speaks of who is not there anymore.

We just know our place. Everybody knows their place. Everybody respects that. That's just the way it is. Its Napoleonic Code here. We don't cross lines here. We respect lines. And that is how we live.

Los Angeles, 1966

The recording artist traveled with his father on his first experience out of Kenner. It had been a long time since his childhood as a sweeper boy in Kenner. They were away from the Gown Men and the Siren. They felt free. They arrived at the hotel in Los Angeles, where he was appearing.

Upon approaching the lobby, he was directed to the rear entrance. Confused, he informed the doorman who he was and that he was scheduled to perform there. He was told that *black folks* did not enter from the front, but through the kitchen.

The doorman was black.

The recording artist's father's eyes welled up with grief. His father said that his sorrow came from the belief that outside of Jefferson Parish, outside of the Gown Men and the Siren, things would be different, they would be free of the thrashing and whipping and tossing. But they were just in another part of America, where nothing changed.

Superstition without insight becomes tradition and perpetuates malice.

Note:

Lloyd Price is an iconic musical artist of the late 1950s who appeared on national television and toured across the country. Among his major hit songs were "Personality," Stagger Lee" and "Wedding Day." He has a treasure of great stories that are funny, poignant, heartbreaking and tragic. He is 85-years old and still performs his act at the Cutting Room in New York City. He introduced the author of this story to the term "Gown Men." This story was written to honor him as a wonderful and dear friend.

The Photo in Your Coat Pocket |
B.J. Fischer

It was the first really nice day of spring. You know the kind of day, the one where you want to unzip your jacket for the first time and feel the cold air upon your chest. The sort when you think maybe you won't need the stocking cap and the gloves and the scarf and the thermal socks again, even though you know you probably will. Anyway, just because you relish the possibility, you go back into the closet and find your Fall-and-Spring coat, your transition coat, your interstitial coat.

You put it on and zip it up about three-quarters of the way and then step outside and it's colder than you thought it was going to be, so you jam your hands into the shallow pockets of the coat.

And that's where you find it. It's a photo of the two of you — you and her — laughing at a party, holding beers. Her brown hair is shiny and thick. You're touching — the two of you — not a lot but a little at the elbow and upper arm and you can feel it now. Still.

Seeing it also makes you want to throw up. Makes it hard to breathe. You want to drop the photo, but you can't.

There's a pumpkin in the background and that makes sense because the photo was in the pocket of your Fall-and-Spring coat. Inside its frame, she's wearing the leather coat she didn't take off at parties. It also had to be about that time of year because you had already gone through the pockets of your winter coat and removed every reminder of her.

And now, this. Now, this.

You haven't been doing much since it had all happened. You work at night, so your days have been spent watching television — old reruns like Dragnet and Zorro —and eating tuna fish and Kraft dinners.

Even though you won't admit it, you try to avoid seeing her. You know where she works, where she goes for lunch and where she shops. You know the roads she uses and where she might be driving or — worse — walking and you avoid those arteries, taking the long ways and the short cuts to avoid being on a thoroughfare of heartbreak.

You are the opposite of a stalker.

And that's what you are supposed to do, right? Mind your own business. Respect her wishes. Let her be.

You are doing that.

You haven't dated much. Some friends tried to fix you up at first, tried to invite you to parties when their cousins from Shaker Heights were visiting or when that new waitress at the restaurant across the street was available after she broke up with a guy who was a jerk and said you'd be a nice change of pace.

You go, you meet them, you say hello, you're polite, but you find that it's pretty easy to softly sabotage this kind of thing by just not trying very hard. A little, but not very hard. It wasn't difficult to make sure nothing happened.

Holding the picture is making you feel different.

You start to walk. You are still avoiding the critical arteries, but you walk along the eastern edge of the neighborhood, which is all wind and flatness. You honestly don't know where you are going. You are just enjoying being outdoors.

You turn and walk along the northern edge, right past the town cemetery, and then you find yourself out past the Applebee's (which used to be a Roy Rogers).

You can see her apartment. It's on the second story of a building with maybe a dozen different units. You walk in that direction — you were headed that way anyway — and pretty soon you are about a hundred feet away, walking in a small warren of similar-sized buildings.

People are out and about, but you are unknown to anyone aside from her and her roommates.

Hiding in plain sight, you walk down the sidewalk on the far side of the parking lot by the building. You can see the curtains — lacy with little red flowers, purchased at a garage sale by her Mom back where they lived, which wasn't here. You remember what they look like from the other side.

You walk by and then you realize it isn't right. What would you say if you were seen? It would be embarrassing. You have no reason to be over there — though you are just walking on a public sidewalk — and she'd wonder why. Or know why, even if it was jumping to a conclusion.

An idea pops into your head.

You could tell her you have a new girlfriend and she lives in the area and you were just visiting her and are now heading back to town. At this hour, she might even think you spent the night. You could show her: you had moved on. Let her see that.

You realize it would be the kind of move people might make as some kind of desperate Hail Mary about two-thirds of the way through a rom-com.

The idea of this does not make you feel good for some reason.

So, you walk away — the long way — around the back of the Catholic Church. You get into a river of humans — women wearing earmuffs to keep their hair right and men without hats at all and everyone with a backpack or a messenger's satchel and no one talking. — and you feel better inside all the bodies jostling their way along the road.

You don't really remember how but you end up at work and you work the night shift: sous chef at a tapas place. Lots of slicing. And you have to make the quince jelly, which is something they had to teach you to do.

It's a long shift. The kitchen is always crazy, and it is good because you don't have time to reflect on anything because you are busy slicing figs. But when the shift ends, and you head outside — it is much colder now, and you wish you had your heavy coat with you — it is like everything is just dumped back onto you, like all the demons come scrambling through the doorway back to you. Your demons like attention — that much has always been clear to you.

You walk back toward her place again. It isn't like before, when you were a human Ouija just wandering and ended up at her building. Now, you are moving with some compulsion. You can do nothing but go there.

When you get there, all is quiet. It's after one in the morning and the building is dark, every single unit. You walk along the sidewalk and you can see that her room is also dark and quiet. No TV glow, no reading lamp. It made sense. She was never the late-night type.

You walk up to the building. The hallways are lit. The outside doors are not locked, never were, and you walk up and put your hand on the big metal handle that is cold with the night and pull it open.

The first thing you notice is the smell. The first thing you know is the smell. It brings back so much to you: nights after dates when you climbed the stairs, your hands softly in the small of her back guiding her to make sure she didn't run away or so she didn't forget you were there and why you were heading home and because you could and it felt good on your hand and radiated up your arm.

The smell is impossible to pick apart. It's warm and musty and smells like under-washed carpet and the purple aggregate of everyone's dinner and late-night tea and cigarette smoke and maybe some lint from the dryer that was running before a tenant went to bed.

It smells like life.

You walk up the stairs. The handrail is thin and metal, and it is connected to their stairs by twisty spindles. You walk softly up the stairs. You know one of the steps squeaks, and you step over it. But, really, who would notice? People were going through all the time. Who could tell when someone might be coming home late or leaving early?

Her apartment was at the top of the stairs just to the left. Number 8. You look at the number on the door, which had always hung a little crooked. It still did. There's a shamrock sticker on the door. You think that maybe they had a St. Patrick's party. You listen. You listen hard. No sound comes from behind her door.

You remember the first time you came to pick her up. Gelatinous with nerves, you knocked on the door. She didn't answer, her roommate did, but you remember walking through the door to wait while she finished getting ready. You remember her wearing a knee-high denim skirt and two-inch heels and a yellow sweater with her thick and shiny brown hair.

And, standing there, you remember every time you entered that door the way a mystic might remember all his previous lives in a glorious instant.

You don't know why, but you pull the picture from your pocket. You look at it again. You and her — happy — with a pumpkin. And you get an idea.

You could just slide the picture under the door. Maybe you could write a note on the back. Hey, thought of you when I saw this picture. Thought maybe you'd want to keep it as . . . as what? A reminder? A keepsake? A memento? A souvenir?

Which brought up a question: had she kept anything from you? Had she stowed anything away, even deep in a drawer, next to that denim skirt, that might someday remind her of the time you spent together?

The question, even unanswered, makes you profoundly sad.

When you first found the photo, you thought that getting rid of it would give you a sense of freedom, liberation, empowerment even. It would be a symbolic completion of what you thought you'd already done, before you saw that wayward, leftover photo in the pocket of your interstitial coat.

The more you think about it, though, the more it makes your pocket feel empty. You could put other things into the pocket if physical emptiness was the issue — maybe a journal or a sketchpad — but you know they would feel foreign, like things that didn't belong there, and you'd still feel the loss.

You put the picture into your pocket and walk back down the stairs and onto the street. It's even colder now, and you really wish you had your warmer coat.

Men Without Hearts, Inc. |
Alex Z. Salinas

They say when you fall in love, you give her a piece of your heart. So when things go bad, and she's gone, you lose a piece of yourself—forever.

I agree with all that except I never *gave* Luz a piece of my heart; no, she *took* it, pillaged the whole beating bleeding thing like a Viqueen. Well, I let her.

My punishment for leaving my chest wide open is living without a heart.

Outside, it's getting dark, raining heavily. The golden hour's fading. The lights are on upstairs, and I'm upstairs sitting on my father's favorite rocking chair. Rocking.

Don't ask if I'm home. The worst question is the kind whose answer is obvious. A purloined letter kind of question.

• • •

When I got a letter in the mail, an invitation/application to join Men Without Hearts, Inc., I was eager to sign up, send them their requested $250 annual club fee. Basically, all the money I had to my name.

If you'll recall, Biggie Smalls once said, "Mo' money, mo' problems." My motto has always been, "No money, no problem!"

The invitation said in two to three months, after payment is received, the club would ship me a piece of some poor sap's chemically treated heart in the form of a pill—a little chewable—so I could feel something, anything, again.

Hooray.

Until then, I had to wander Earth without a core.

Without a ticker to match the rhythm of my footsteps, or at the very least provide me a beat to tap my foot to, time was relative, irrelevant—yesterday's newspaper in the hands of an actuary.

In other words, I had all the time in the world, and nowhere to dump it.

• • •

I miss her body, the way she filled out her Levi's, the way she let me slide my hands under her blouse, run my greedy fingers up and down her dark curves, lick her salty-sweet Luz skin, give her goosebumps.

I miss her mind, that shadowy jungle, the way Luz chuckled at kids in restaurants choking on food—naughty girl—and the way she got dead-serious gazing at lonely old men in diners shuffle off to the restroom. "Their time's up, baby, and ours has just beguneth," I'd tell her in these saturated situations. She'd look at me with slatted eyes, blazing lips, and respond with something to the tune of, "You talk like an amateur hedonist, honey, a boy who's yet to grow into his own fur." My arms and legs were only mildly hairy.

I had to admit: the girl was deep.

I miss her farts, silent but deadly, always while I drove, always her devilish grin a sign of her guilt.

I miss her smile, her straight white teeth—her long thin neck I could wrap my hands around, gently.

I miss being King of her Mind, Body & Soul. My one true Queen.

Luz.

• • •

It's been four months and still no package. I'm obsessed with waiting for the mail. I can tell that Daryl, my postman, is frightened to death of me. He probably wishes I were dead. Some days I think I am. It could be my breath. Brushing my teeth again, flossing, might help my case. Listerine strips, too, if I could afford them.

It could also be the gaping hole in my chest, the very wound Daryl was transfixed by.

"This?" I said, thumbing to it. "This is just a significant chasm in my center. An empty tomb. You can poke it if you want. It doesn't really hurt anymore."

"You craycee, mayne, you craycee," Daryl said, taking a step backwards.

"Why Dare-Dare," I said, stepping toward him, reaching out to pat his shoulder.

"Don't you touch me, craycee mayne!"

Yet my palm had already found its desired destination.

• • •

Five months.

I've been ripped off. Scammed. There's no magical capsule coming. I'm a victim of my own problems—of hoaxes, schemes, conspiracies and pilfered adoration.

I must wander this earth without a core. That's my punishment.

Ever heard of Hammurabi's Code? Universal law? Karmic justice? Cosmic indifference? Chaos theory?

Yeah, yeah, yeah. Hate to break it to you, sweetie, but those are just fancy labels for "Tough fucking luck."

• • •

Six months.

Wandering.

Broke.

Broke and heartless. Heartless and broke—don't know which combination sounds better.

My beard is big and poofy. My body's skinny, twig-like, stinks something awful too, according to the masses.

What's my age again? I don't remember. It's easier to forget than you think.

What's there left to register?

Aha, registers! Ka-ching.

I could have all the money and jewels in the world, but still no core. No Luz.

Cold. I'm very cold.

Did I mention it barely stopped raining this morning?

Today, I met some kids at the park. They stared at my chest, seemed impressionable enough within my purview.

"There's nothing there for you to see, children, so look into my eyes!" I shouted. "Here's your lesson for today: When heartless, hold on tight to your money!"

They all made like sissy bananas and split.

Me, I stayed put, looked up at the sky, spotted the sun peeking out of the clouds finally.

"Hey there, Mr. Sol," I announced. "It's good to see you, been a while."

Then it hit me: Talking warmed me up, replaced stagnant vapors in my body with a fresh breeze as though the ocean was around the corner. It was exactly what the doctor had ordered, and it felt incredible—felt incredible to feel incredible!

Now I just needed to recalibrate my inside-voice. Tackle one problem at a time. Yeah. That was plenty of work to keep a mere mortal busy.

ESSAYS

A School Board Meeting Challenges Faith | Bekah S. McNeel

Recently I covered what has been by far the most difficult events of my young journalism career: a school board meeting. I'm an education reporter, and school board meetings feature regularly my calendar. Usually the primary challenge is staying awake.

On that Monday night, the primary challenge was keeping my faith.

In August 2017, San Antonio Independent School District added sexual orientation and gender identity to its non-discrimination policy. The policy had been in place for decades, with race, gender, religion and other standard non-discrimination language included. Given the likelihood of bullying and employment discrimination toward LGBTQIA people, the school board decided to do what other major cities have done and add that population to the policy.

Shortly thereafter, a group of Christians began to mobilize to protest. Wearing "school bus yellow" the group flooded the SAISD board, claiming to be concerned for the rights of those girls who would be "traumatized" by seeing boys in their restrooms and made broad statements about sexual promiscuity, predation and protecting innocence. They also invoked God's name as they demanded that the district institute an "immutable gender" policy.

In the week leading up to the meeting, word had spread about the protest, and LGBTQIA activist groups began to mobilize. When I arrived at the board meeting, there were 300 people packed into a room that comfortably holds around 100. Forty-nine people signed up to speak during citizens-to-be-heard. Usually, there are fewer than ten people.

Throughout the process, representatives from either side of the ideological aisle approached the microphone to cheers from their compatriots, who stood in the back waving signs that said either "God Created 2 Genders: Male and Female" or "Protect LGBTQIA Students."

Both sides held signs. Both spoke passionately. Only one side misbehaved. Those who were there explicitly claiming to be doing God's business by calling for the repeal of the non-discrimination policy were raucous and rude. They shouted over the speakers and booed gay teenagers who were there to say "thank you" to the school board for the new language in the non-discrimination policy. They yelled at the school board president (a Catholic urban missionary who has taken a vow of poverty to live deep on our city's Westside and minister to her neighborhood), saying that she is untrustworthy and disrespectful.

With exactly two exceptions, those expressing support for the policy did not shout. They did not "boo." They left the podium when their time was up.

I won't go into the fearmongering, pseudoscience and invocation of the judgment of God. That all happened, too, and it was painful.

Teenagers heard adults call them mentally ill, depraved and suggest that they were only gay or transgender because their parents had neglected them.

One woman, wearing a Christian T-shirt, shouted that transgender students didn't deserve to be protected.

Students were crying. Their parents, far from neglectful, were furious.

After accusing the school board of being covert and sneaky, the protestors excused themselves from the very public forum in which such decisions are made. The school board went about its live-streamed business in front of the sparse crowd that remained, fully transparent, just like they were on the day the policy passed.

Christians, we cannot just show up when there's a battle we feel like fighting. If the school board is your battlefield, you need to be at every meeting. The teacher's union is there. Representatives from the mayor's office are there. Where are we, church?

If you are one of those Christians reading this and saying, "The media always focuses on the extreme Christians . . ." I ask again, where are *you*? Where are you, reasonable Christians, when I'm taking quotes and begging you to go on record and speak up for the Gospel?

Later, on the steps of the SAISD administration building, the pastor leading the protest said, "We don't hate the LGBT community just because we believe there are only two genders."

The students gathered didn't buy that logic. Not after what they had just heard inside. That same pastor had implied that they were predators, boys masquerading as girls for nefarious purposes, including "recruiting kindergarteners."

Into my camera students expressed, with great clarity, the church's major roadblock in reaching the transgender community: the church won't admit that they exist.

Conservative Christians are sending the message loudly and clearly: we can't minister to your soul until we fix your sexuality. Until then, you are dead to us. Your feelings don't matter. You don't even exist.

The tough reality for the church, is that transgender people *do* exist. We should consider the possible consequences of writing off an entire segment of humanity.

I have never been more sympathetic with the heterosexuals who leave the church over this issue. I have never wanted to be less identified with my brothers and sisters.

Two things kept me in the church on Monday night:

First, my entire worldview does not hang on society's acceptance or rejection of gay marriage. It's an issue the church can work through; we don't have to come to peace about it today. We're starting in a pretty polarized place, and we need to have some tough conversations, but I think we can bear with each other.

I believe that Jesus brings hope for the LGBTQIA community. Not hope that one day they can be heterosexual. Hope that they can know the same peace, acceptance and love that I have found, because they need Jesus just like I do. Not because of their sexual identity, but because of their humanity.

The other thing that kept me in the church was the work of a single pastor. The one evangelical pastor who showed up, not to speak from the podium, but to move around the room hugging students, telling them God loves them and letting them know that he was there to listen if they ever wanted to talk about faith.

Virginity | Jeri Griffith

I.

"Are you a virgin?"

The two boys leer at me. Their silly grins hide something that, to me, is inscrutable. I don't know if I'm a virgin or not.

I'm not sure what I should say. I feel there's some trick here. If I say yes, I might be caught. They will know I'm not sure what they're talking about. If I say no, that could be the wrong answer. Heads or tails? Yes or no?

I pause to squint wisely, gazing across the school ground where other children are playing kickball.

"Sure," I reply, "Sure, I'm a virgin."

Donnie Mayer rolls his eyes and turns to Larry Kaminski to laugh.

With the thumb and index finger of his left hand, he makes a circle. Then he sticks the middle finger of his right hand inside it, moving it up and down through the hole. He smiles again, a slightly evil smile, then snorts through his nose as if this were the funniest thing in the world.

My face must register a blankness I wish I could hide. Larry flushes and looks away, seemingly embarrassed. I stare down at the ground wondering exactly why they are picking on me.

That afternoon, Donny passes me a note during the geography lesson. I LOVE YOU is printed in big, crude, irregular letters. I turn my head to glance at him. He's pretending not to notice me. I stuff the note into my geography book.

The next day, I get another note. This one is from Larry. Again, it says I LOVE YOU. Inside the paper, I find a ring from a Cracker Jack box. I recognize it as the same prize I got two weeks ago.

More happens.

Larry and Donny begin walking me home at lunchtime. They wait outside on the street for me. After two or three days, they have a fight. They walk down the block and tussle in the tall grass next to the railroad tracks. Larry seems to have won because, when they reappear, Donny's face is scratched and bleeding. They're fighting over which of them is going to marry me. When they return from this exchange of fisticuffs, they seem to have agreed to disagree.

Donny says "screw." He says it over and over. "Screw you. Screw."

Both of them seem to think this is very funny just to say the word again and again. I don't get it. Why are they picking on me and what do they want? I honestly don't know.

II.

In *The Wounded Angel,* Finnish artist Hugo Simberg depicts small white flowers blundering forth under a steely sky. A shrub in the background shows yellow buds, but there is little sign of greenery so it must be early spring. In this 1903 oil painting, two boys utilize a makeshift stretcher to transport their cargo—a child angel with flaxen hair dressed in radiantly white clothing. The angel's drooping head is bound with a cloth that partially hides her face and covers her eyes. Her cream-colored wings, rendered useless by some invisible wound, drape listlessly.

The young lad at the front of their procession has donned a black suit and derby. His dark shoes look too large for him. With eyes intent on the path, he exudes an exceedingly somber demeanor. The expression on his cohort's face could be construed as a mixture of guilt, sadness, and anger. There's some sense here that, although the boys rescued the angel, they might also be the ones who wounded her.

Barely able to support herself in an upright position, the angel seems ready to go wherever the boys are taking her. The scene is sad, and the boys seem penitent. We don't know what has happened in the last hours or what the future might hold. The angel is injured. Some fall has occurred, and they are all three of them deciding what to do about it.

III.

I am an eleven-year-old girl with blonde hair and blue eyes. I am not an angel. I'm earthbound, and more often than not, instead of dreaming of flying, I dream of falling. The same dream recurs to disrupt my sleep. Granted bird's-eye vision, I peer over the edge of my mattress to see a crisscross of roads and farm fields far below me. Still high in the air, this bed is a safe berth, but the pull of gravity is inexorable. I plunge toward those fields. I'm going to die. My life as I have known it is about to end. Waking, I pant with fear, but I don't know what I'm afraid of.

IV.

In Paul Gauguin's painting, *The Loss of Virginity*, a naked girl-child lies exposed in the foreground next to some gray rocks. A reddish-brown dog sports a rakish, almost human expression as he presides over the girl's body with one paw placed between her breasts. The girl's pale, prone form echoes the shape of the landscape. Why is she unclothed and exposed in this forlorn place where red earth meets a sky of thin clouds? There's something ominous going on here. By title, the painter tells us that the image is about the girl's loss of virginity. Faceless villagers in a distant line wend along a dirt road. The girl's connection to these fellow humans is unclear.

V.

Finally, the falling dream reaches its conclusion. I am lying on my back in the middle of a cornfield. I have come down to earth and I am not dead. The dizzying descent is over. I have my first menstrual period. Nothing has changed and yet everything has changed. Boys become a part of my life. In high school, I go steady with a different boy each year. I wear class rings wrapped with yarn to make them stay on my finger. I go around in my guy's letter jacket. I stay out until the wee hours on the night of the prom. I experience all the drama and excitement of fighting off advances while making out in the back seats of cars.

All these cultural markers eventually lead to the day when I lose my virginity. I'm no longer a girl living at home. I'm away at school. The boy has been pressuring me for months. It's what he wants more than anything else. On my part, I am just tired, tired of putting up resistance. I agree. We use a condom, and it's over very quickly.

The next day, I find myself walking across the college campus in springtime. Huge trees spread their leafing branches above me. A robin hopping on the grassy lawn cocks its head to listen for the telltale worm. I feel proud of myself, as though I've passed some secret milestone that no one else can see. Inwardly, I smile. But did I conquer or was I merely conquered? I don't know. I feel the indifferent villagers in Gauguin's painting walking wordlessly away.

Soon after, I end my relationship with that boy. The following spring brings a major update. I've fallen for someone new. He's a writer. We read books together. We talk about feelings and about everything there is to talk about in the world. And we don't have sex. We make love.

VI.

It's May and the redbuds are blooming. I'm headed toward the house of Winifred Van Etten, a professor emeritus from the small college I attend who has become a friend. She's in her seventies and retired now, but she taught English at the college for decades. Years ago, in 1936, Winifred won the *Atlantic Monthly* prize for her book *I am the Fox*. It's a novel, yes, but in many ways, also a feminist text.

A redhead when she was young, Winifred must have equated herself with the fox, the terrified object of the hunt desperately trying to escape the hunters. She did not wish to be pursued and subdued by any man. She did not want to be demeaned or held back because she was a woman. In Ben Van Etten, she found a companion who treated her as an equal. He allowed her the freedom she needed to be herself. They had no children.

I find Winifred sitting on the walkway next to the stone house she and Ben built all those years ago with prize money generated by the novel. She's combing out her long, white hair, drying it in the sun. Usually she wears it up so I've never seen her like this before. Now she is old, and she's no longer the fox flashing red in front of the hounds. I approach to sit on the stone stairs beside her.

Winifred is not like other people. She sees no reason to make conversation when there's nothing to say. Sometimes, we sit silently for twenty minutes and then she'll comment on a bird or tell a story about her dog, Jolie, who is long dead. She has survived two cancers. She has known two world wars. She is for women's rights and opposed to all kinds of violence. Sometimes, she sighs dejectedly and says reflectively: "Ah, well, the men will have their toys and they must play with them." By this, she means weapons. She means wars.

I think Winifred knows I am not a virgin. But we don't talk about that. She touches the stump of the grapevine that had to be cut down last year. It was becoming unmanageable and overgrowing the path. The grape wood was thick as my wrist. When burned in the fireplace, it gave off of a particularly bright and intense flame. All things burn in the end. The grape vine is cut down. The girl-child loses her virginity and her innocence. The hours of an old woman's life waver like a candle flame. Winifred continues combing her white hair.

"I have to go now," I say. "I've got studying to do."

PAINTINGS

Liberals | Brianna Keeper

Liberals Arts Building
The University of Texas at Austin
20x16
Acrylic on canvas
2003

Big Lafayette | Brianna Keeper

Lafayette Park
San Francisco, California
Acrylic on canvas
2003

Firehole Canyon | Brianna Keeper

Yellowstone National Park
Wyoming
20x16,
Acrylic on canvas
2003

MORE POETRY

Don't Wake Me Up, Just Yet |
Mike James

It's the dream where I recite my social security number forwards and backward before I can have sex. Isn't that a pain? The sex robot is accommodating and hints at numbers I stumble over like a teenager running late for class. I always like hints. They are one of my favorite things after Julie Andrews, long walks, big bands, and dark chocolates (the healthy kind.) Does that sound like the personal ad so many poems are? Oh, well. We are all looking for someone even if it ends up being a cat on the windowsill, taking in every bit of sun a room allows. In this case, those aren't the devil, dismissive pair of cat eyes I'm used to. It's ok, though. I'm not afraid. I was trying to not make this about who isn't in the dream. No such-and-such lurch for this old cowboy. I tripped on my boots and fell and fell. Did I mention, the hallway is empty? A band is playing somewhere.

OCD | Joshua Lindenbaum

OCD (Oh-see-dee) n. 1. An imagination that can override trusting one's self. 2. Checking the doorknob for the eighth time because you know that if you don't, it's going to bother you; *what if someone walks in and steals everything?; what if I didn't lock it and my family is killed, and it would be* my *fault? I would never get over the guilt. And if I couldn't get over the guilt, then I might…*
3. Hovering your hand over the doorknob. 4. Repetitive thoughts that make brainwashers dry heave. 5. Turning the car around to make sure that pothole wasn't a person. *If it was a person, I think I would've noticed; I was looking right at the road (after all).* 6. Logic often loses. 7. A friend asks to try your drink and a montage of diseases and germs scroll past your eyes. 8. Your hands beg for mercy when they see the sink again. 9. Projecting your thoughts onto to others, an empathy without empathy for one's self. 10. Pain. Lots. 11. Treatment is available; there is hope. 12. It won't be easy.
OCD (Oh-see-dee) adj. 1. The act of describing a quirk or ritual as in *I have to make sure all of my shoes are facing forward; I'm sooo OCD.* 2. If you ever made a similar statement, refer to noun.
3. Would you like to rephrase your statement?

After Kevin Coval and A. Van Jordan

Sanctuary | James H. Duncan

there is a small hill near my father's home
in San Antonio where a single
lamppost spreads a golden circle
into the night just barely catching
all four corners of the silent
residential intersection, all homes
dark, all streets empty, palms
and salt grass cutting jagged edges
into the midnight dark, reminding
me of same such quiet walks in
Los Angeles towns in outlying
hills, of the sunsets in San Francisco
too, and sometimes writer friends
would quote Kerouac
and his California dispatches, but
on any given night when words appear
through the midnight filter, I am
there on that small hill
with the orange dome over the far
downtown San Antonio skyline,
a color matching my lamppost sanctuary,
with a breeze that comes
and dies with a cat watching
from the darkened alley
and then car headlights cut through and
footsteps take me to where the city fades
beneath the wild oak canopy, the
dark of life taking hold again,
sending me home with whispers
and enticements of bars and women,
of scars and laughter and loneliness,
of traffic in the distance and leaves on the ground,
a dead city jazz playing for you and me

Reprinted from the book Dead City Jazz *with permission.*

Sister Cities | Abby Mangel

I love you, Kumamoto.
But my missions are in a state of decay.
The limestone aqueducts, once traversing proudly alongside the Piedras Creek, the ones that pumped crystalline liquid into the mouths of my native born children, are dried.
They too have crumbled under the heat of June air raids; they are mercury to the touch.
A foolish child even took a knife and scrawled into my mossy contoured places, 'Great Tit!'
Yes, I have since relinquished my walls to such awful graffiti, so crass, so thoughtless—
But I know that you would cackle at the irony, Kumamoto, like a perching songbird with a green breast.
Your laughter was always an alarm call, but your hilltop castles from the sixteenth century tower above this smut and gunfire, impregnable.
I see the bombs descending upon my palm-lined streets, but I know they first touched down upon your distant pavements;
Our mutual calamity became the center that holds us together, our scarred and sunken ground zero.
Dirty needles and cigarette buds people my gutters, but blackened children line yours under cherry blossoms.
The same coordinates where a silver plane dropped an inferno onto your hot pink camellia flowers also was where a calico cat named Rita lighted its bushy tail on a burning candlewick, dissolving into the fierce southwestern sunshine,
All while its careless owner took a siesta and dreamt of deer leaping over a wire fence.
Now, that's what I call some hot pussy, Kumamoto!
The earthquakes rage, but I love you still.
—San Antone

June 25th | Rudy Martinez

Tuesday, 25th of June 2019. Bushwick, Brooklyn.
Three or four times a week, I go to a Puerto Rican restaurant called La Isla. On the days I don't order half a rotisserie chicken with yellow rice and black beans, I get pork
with yellow rice and black beans.
Today, I got the pork.
I got the pork after calling my mother to ask her how many times a week I should eat pork.
I trust my mother's advice over a doctor's.
She said three-to-four times a week is fine, especially since I'm active and the pork isn't fried.
My mother yawned four times during our eight-minute conversation, so I said goodbye after we
briefly discussed a picture of drowned migrants, a young father and daughter, that the world was
witness to today.
I walked to La Isla, trying to wrap my head around what it is like to drown during a desperate
attempt to reach the greatest imperial power to ever exist.
After ordering pork with yellow rice and black beans, the gentleman to my right received half a
rotisserie chicken with white rice and red beans.
He moved the plate of chicken closer and bowed his head, presumably to pray.
I watched him pray.
I watched him pray and pray and pray for about 30 seconds as his food cooled down.
Seeing him pray, deferring the instant gratification chicken, white rice, and red beans can
bring, was inspiring.
When it came my time to receive a slightly different plate of food, the ideal being similar (meat
as the centerpiece with rice and beans playing parts in an ever-reliable supporting cast), I
would pray, too.
This guy knew nothing about me. He'd find my prayer authentic.
I'd even silently count to thirty, just for added measure.

The woman who brought my plate over asked if I wanted anything to drink and I said no; she
walked away before I could ask for limes and hot sauce.
Fuck.
Time to pray.
I moved the plate of pork closer and bowed my head to pray.
My eyes were closed, and as I counted to thirty all I could think of was that picture.
Two migrants, a young father and his daughter, drowned, discovered face down on the shores of
the Rio Grande.
When my time was up, I slowly raised my head and looked forward in contempt.
I don't know what I hated more: the gentleman to my right, his material conditions, my light
skin, ICE agents, an amalgamation of all these things, or something else, something
indescribable.
Imagine what it's like to have someone to thank, to blame, to beg —
someone besides oneself.
I wanted to ask the gentleman to my right what had occurred during his prayer.
Did he thank god for his food?
Maybe he prayed for open borders or the rise of a legitimate people's party?
I wanted to ask the gentleman to my right to estimate how many times he prays a week,
confirm that each of his prayers lasts around 30 seconds,
and then ask how long he's been praying.
Let's do some math.
After reaching a sum, I'd pull a page from my pocket notebook and scribble the sum on it, in
somewhat messy block lettering.
Keep this, I'd tell him.
Add to it every time you pray.
You'd think I'd walk out after that, but I'd still have food to finish, pork with yellow rice and
black beans.
So, I'd go back to minding my own business.

a cynic is a man | David Matthews

... in the marketplace of ideas what currency is in use
what now-ness affords
anything
A cynic is a man
sold
as-is
an idea purchase on the slippery
ain't
slope
what inclination feeds

a frenzy of consumption *perverts* / *distorts* / Good Salesmanship
who knows T.B.he price *mis-represents* / *exaggerates*
or not T.B. *mis-states*
? dismisses
When *disregards, disses*
is the truth SO un- the
as- cost / benefit
of everything sal- ratio
able (see-worthy)
that it can be marked down
— a volumn discount —
by the manus (seismic) factor
the-value-added-by-the- a profit
and the value hand-of-man without
the product oner
packaged in his own
matured-and- made-palatable Cuntery
for shipment... aggregated and
so am i
of Nothing
That Wilde man

Feeding the Fish | Rebecca Schumejda

The lone algae eater, who somehow
survives our neglect, hides inside a castle.
When I tap the glass to see if he's
still alive, I think about my little brother,
who spends twenty-three hours a day
confined to a 6 by 8 cell. When I open
the top and sprinkle in food, the fish
rises up through the murky water to eat.

Visiting him means leaving my feelings
behind, passing through metal detectors
and multiple check points, so I can
sit across from someone I don't know
if I ever knew. I buy him vending machine
food and rise up through the murky water
to eat. While we play cards, I watch him
transform — lungs to gills, arms to fins,

skin to scales. We are mostly silent
as he extracts oxygen from water,
but when I finally speak to him, it's like
how I talk to the algae eater when I
open up the lid of the tank, *Listen*, I say,
even though I don't do it often, I am
the only one who feeds you anymore,
how are you still alive, seriously, how?

Sunny Lake Crazy | Rex Wilder

The absent-minded
Looks sheeting the nurses'
Faces are blasphemous
Here at sunny Lake Crazy.
I am condescended to
Like a walking diaper
At best, except it's my head
That's incontinent.
This woman, if I flirt
With her now, it'd
Be like the old man
In the wheelchair
Who pinches the nurse's
Ass. For all I know
I'm limp all over.
She'd slap my wrist
While looking
At her watch & enter
The incident in her log.
I can't even get
A pity face this morning.
Not even from
The man in the mirror.

White with a Little Shade | Joel Fry

She was a white girl, to be precise,
with black hair, who never said anything,
but walked ahead of me in the fog—
this girl like me—who was taken from my reflection—
a face so bright it shone like the moon.

There was a warm place then, with no words.
We lived there together.

Duh—duh—duh—DAY
Duh—duh—duh—DAY—DAY—DAY
Duh—duh—duh—DAY
Duh—duh—duh—DAY—DAY—DAY

That was my soul too—a spicy Creole jazz
that can be eaten with a spoon—
a light not seen since August
that permeated the locks of my curly hair.

She featured herself in this light,
resplendent in the crushed glow of velvet.
She knew how to transform the streets
we walked down to a letter sounding
in the night.

I enjoyed her world and mine together,
her voice as dark as molasses
I dipped my tongue into.

A Teacher's Hope: Being Remembered | David A. Grenardo

How do you want to be remembered by your students? And, more importantly, when?

For your awards or accolades and only at the end?

In some big ceremony, retirement, or a funeral attended by many,

Which of those ways do I want to be remembered by my students? Not any.

I want to be remembered during certain times by those whose lives I've touched;

I want my students to remember me and to understand I've loved them so much.

When a former student is sad, I want him to remember a joke I told him and laugh;

When a former student is weak, she remembers my words or deeds and her problem she attacks;

When a former student is treated badly, I want him to treat others with dignity and respect;

When a former student has the chance to be a hero, I want her to do what I expect;

And when a former student feels alone, I want him to ask for peace,

Because God is always with us, the greatest and the least.

I want to be remembered in ways that empower the students I've known,

For that means I truly helped them and through my teaching they have grown.

Neptune's Son | Daniel Edward Moore

Last night, a boy again,
    fell from Ohio's steamy sky,
        shedding his ivory northwest skin

  into Appalachia's coal-stained hands
      on the river's muddy arms.
          It took Alaska's steel grey wings

to lamp his face with fireflies.
    Morse code flashed above cottonmouths
        cruising the creek for dinner

as frogs folded their legs in prayer,
    sparing themselves from a three-prong gig,
        dripping with summer's hunger.

This is why Neptune's son,
    wounded the side of a hill with forts,
        his ribs splayed by a rocky world

nothing red & beating could save,
    nothing compared to the floodwall's face
        washed in the beauty of time.

Bending Time | Jennifer R. Lloyd

Where'd you learn to bend time like that?

You found the portal on instinct.

Our two mouths like black holes connecting,

Lips and teeth and tongue marking

The fissure where solid time turns liquid,

Where night stretches

In communion with parked cars,

Where street dogs gather their feast,

Where we gather our longing

And pass it back and forth,

Like the best ball game ever played,

Where your hands find what they demand,

Palms buried deep in my hair,

Where my eyes find what they seek,

Locked on yours, dazed and dopey,

Where you steal my breath,

And give me yours in exchange,

And we call it even.

    Where'd you learn to bend time like that?

        Here, in the hidden life of parking lots.

ALL GOOD THINGS

Read | Listen | Watch

Staff suggestions.

A Zero-Sum Game by Eduardo Rabasa

Oval by Elvia Wilk

Riots I Have Known by Ryan Chapman

Tears of the Trufflepig: A Novel by Fernando A. Flores

Revenge of the Translator by Brice Matthieussent

Red Plenty by Francis Spufford

Miss Lonelyhearts by Nathanael West

Amulet by Roberto Bolaño

Gun, With Occasional Music by Jonathan Lethem

Deep Vellum Publishing

Open Letter Books

Interpreting the Masters, Volume 2: (A Tribute to Van Halen) by the bird and the bee

Love in the Time of E-Mail by Antarctigo Vespucci

Howdy High-Rise by Croy and the Boys

The Family on Netflix

Coffee House Press

inadequate.net

Quotes

"To describe new varieties of good and evil – there lies the great task of the writer." —Adam Zagajewski

"Our wealth must be spiritual, and we must content ourselves with smalls sips while others choke on prosperity." —Salvator Rosa

"But where do survivors
Find the strength to
Endure such violent
Revisions of reality?" —Ron Padgett, "Completion," *Big Cabin*

"He talked about how difficult life was here, but he rarely mentioned having any regret, which made her think that perhaps he regretted it all." —Melissa Rivero, *The Affairs of the Falcons*

"Philanthropy is the cornerstone of neoliberalism . . ."

"And how neoliberal! It's just an acceleration of what's already in place. You relocate responsibility for handling human problems from governments to corporations, then you let corporations pass it off to individuals by shaming them."

"Nonprofit is now officially a subsidiary of profit, just like it always was." —Elvia Wilk, *Oval*

"They were the kind of people who had been through a lot of shit together and were trying, every day, to make that into a strength rather than a weakness." —Jake Wolff, *The History of Living Forever*

"Such is the spirit of the human heart: where it finds the most resistance, it is there that it tends to put the most effort."
—Rodrigo Rey Rose, *Human Matters*

"Someone once said that it is easier to imagine the end of the world than to imagine the end of capitalism."
—Fredric Jameson, "Future City," *New Left Review*

Contributors

Michelle Brooks' *work has been published or is forthcoming in* Threepenny Review, Alaska Quarterly Review, Iowa Review, Hayden's Ferry Review, Natural Bridge *and elsewhere. Her poetry collection,* Make Yourself Small, *was published by Backwaters Press, and her novella,* Dead Girl, Live Boy, *was published by Storylandia Press.*

Born and raised in the Woodlawn Lake area of San Antonio, **Diane Gonzales Bertrand**'s *first book of poetry,* Dawn Flower *(2013) earned special recognition from the Texas Writers League. Her new collection,* The Taco Magician and Other Poems for Kids / El mago de los tacos y otros poemas para niños, *arrives in bookstores November 2019. Bertrand has been published in* The Texas Poetry Calendar *and* VIA Poetry on the Move. *In 2018, she was named a city Tricentennial Poet. As Writer-in-Residence at St. Mary's University, Bertrand teaches composition and creative writing in the English Literature and Language Department.*

Bekah McNeel *is a native San Antonian and journalist. Mother of two, wife of one and reader of many, Bekah is constantly exploring with books and kids in tow.*

Abby Mangel *is a graduate of the English Language and Literature Master's Program at St. Mary's University. She earned a Bachelor of Arts with a double major in English and philosophy from Trinity University. She is a rock n' roll journalist, and she completed her Master's Thesis on Bob Dylan.*

Jennifer R. Lloyd *is a former journalist and longtime logophile. No longer churning words into newsprint on the daily, she sweats out the demons in South Texas or purges them onto the page. In her spare time, she accumulates college degrees and explores poetry and fiction.*

Emma Lee's *most recent collection is* Ghosts in the Desert *(IDP, UK 2015).* The Significance of a Dress *is forthcoming from Arachne Press (UK). She co-edited* Over Land, Over Sea *(Five Leaves, UK, 2015) and reviews for* The Blue Nib, High Window Journal, The Journal, London Grip *and* Sabotage Reviews.

Rebecca Schumejda *is the author of several full-length collections including* Falling Forward *(sunnyoutside press),* Cadillac Men *(NYQ Books),* Waiting at the Dead End Diner *(Bottom Dog Press) and, most recently,* Our One-Way Street *(NYQ Books). She is currently working on a book forthcoming from Stubborn Mule Press. She is the co-editor at* Trailer Park Quarterly. *She received her MA in Poetics from San Francisco State University and her BA from SUNY New Paltz. She lives in New York's Hudson Valley with her family.*

Brittany Leitner *is a journalist and poet living in New York City and originally from San Antonio, Texas. Her articles and poems have been published in* Bustle, Elite Daily, No Dear, Palette Poetry, The Write Launch *and elsewhere. Poems from her 2018 chapbook* 23 Emotions *have won the Sequestrum new writer award, the International Merit Award from the* Atlanta Review *and third place in the 2018 Palette Poetry Prize judged by Shane McCrae.*

Writer and artist ***Jeri Griffith*** *lives and works in Brattleboro, Vermont, after stints in Boston and Austin, Texas, but her childhood was spent in Wisconsin. These disparate places each feel like separate countries to her, with landscapes, seasons and ways of being that influence both her art and her identity. Jeri has published stories and essays in literary quarterlies. She is currently working on a memoir and a collection of short stories, as well as organizing exhibitions of her art.*

Rudy Martinez *is the son of Colombian immigrants and a graduate of Texas State University. He currently resides in Brooklyn, New York.*

David A. Grenardo *is a tenured professor of law at the St. Mary's University School of Law in San Antonio.*

Luke Neftali Villafranca *is a graduate of St. Mary's University. He is a writer and a boxer.*

Rex Wilder *has published poetry in* Poetry *(Chicago),* TLS *(London),* The Nation, The National Review, The New Republic, Yale Review, Harvard Review, Antioch Review, Ploughshares *and many anthologies. Rex has published four books.*

James H. Duncan is the editor of Hobo Camp Review and the author of Feral Kingdom, Nights Without Rain, and We Are All Terminal But This Exit Is Mine, *among other collections of poetry and fiction. He is a former editor with* Writer's Digest, *a columnist for* FIVE:2:ONE *and he writes reviews of independent bookshops at* The Bookshop Hunter.

Mike James has been widely published in magazines throughout the country. His thirteen poetry collections include: Jumping Drawbridges in Technicolor *(Blue Horse),* First-Hand Accounts from Made-Up Places *(Stubborn Mule),* Crows in the Jukebox *(Bottom Dog),* My Favorite Houseguest *(FutureCycle), and* Peddler's Blues *(Main Street Rag.) He has served as an associate editor for the* Kentucky Review *and Autumn House Press, as well as the publisher of the now-defunct* Yellow Pepper Press. *He makes his home outside Nashville, Tennessee.*

Kevin Ridgeway is the author of Too Young to Know *(Stubborn Mule Press). His work has recently appeared in* Slipstream, Chiron Review, Nerve Cowboy, Main Street Rag, The American Journal of Poetry, The Cape Rock, Trailer Park Quarterly *and* So it Goes: The Literary Journal of the Kurt Vonnegut Memorial Library. *He lives and writes in Long Beach, California.*

B. J. Fischer has been published in PIF Magazine, The View From Here, *the* Linden Avenue Literary Journal *and* Blue Lake Review. *His essays have appeared in* The Fiddleback, Ardor, The (Toledo) Blade, the Bygone Bureau, Punchnel's, Thought Catalog, Impose Magazine, the Minneapolis Review of Baseball, midmajority.com *and* Ontologica.

John Bonanni spent a career in the theatre on tour, on Broadway, at Radio City Musical Hall and many places in between managing every sensitive personality he encountered. He now writes about them, among other things. He has been published in Adelaide Literary Magazine, Senior Outlook, Poor Yorick Literary Journal *and* Inspired Magazine. *He will complete the MFA program in Creative and Professional Writing at Western Connecticut State University in 2019.*

John Sweet's recent collections include Heathen Tongue *(Kendra Steiner Editions) and* Bastard Faith *(Scars Publications).*

Larry Smith *is a poet, fiction writer and biographer of Lawrence Ferlinghetti and Kenneth Patchen. His most recent work is* Thoreau's Lost Journal: Poems *and* Tu Fu Comes to America. *He's a professor emeritus of Bowling Green State University in Ohio and director of Bottom Dog Press. He and his wife live along the shores of Lake Erie in Ohio.*

David M. Taylor's *work has appeared in various magazines, such as* Albany Poets, Califragile, Misfit Magazine, Rat's Ass Review *and* Trailer Park Quarterly. *He was also a finalist for the 2017 Annie Menebroker Poetry Award, and his most recent poetry chapbook,* Growing Up Black, *was published by CWP Collective Press.*

Luis Cuauhtémoc Berriozábal *was born in Mexico and lives in Los Angeles, California, where he works in the mental health field. His latest chapbook,* Make the Light Mine, *was published by Kendra Steiner Editions. His first poetry book,* Raw Materials, *was published by Pygmy Forest Press.*

Jesse Breite's *recent poetry has appeared in* Spillway, Crab Orchard Review, Terrain, *and* Prairie Schooner. *His chapbook,* The Knife Collector, *was published in 2013, and he is an associate editor for* The Good Works Review. *He is also librettist for three of Atlanta composer Michael Kurth's scores. Jesse teaches high school English in Atlanta where he lives with his wife and son.*

Charlie Brice *is the author of* Flashcuts Out of Chaos *(2016),* Mnemosyne's Hand *(2018) and* An Accident of Blood *(2019), all from WordTech Editions. His poetry has been nominated for the Best of Net anthology and twice for a Pushcart Prize and has appeared in* The Atlanta Review, The Main Street Rag, Chiron Review, Fifth Wednesday Journal, The Paterson Literary Review *and elsewhere.*

Ace Boggess *is author of four books of poetry, most recently* I Have Lost the Art of Dreaming It So *(Unsolicited Press, 2018) and* Ultra Deep Field *(Brick Road Poetry Press, 2017). His writing appears in* Notre Dame Review, Rhino, North Dakota Quarterly, Rattle *and many other journals. He received a fellowship from the West Virginia Commission on the Arts and spent five years in a West Virginia prison. He lives in Charleston, West Virginia.*

Joel Fry *lives in Athens, Alabama. His poetry can be read online at* Eclectica, Gravel, Ghost Town, The Avatar Review *and on his blog,* Susurrus Waking.

Daniel Edward Moore *lives in Washington on Whidbey Island with the poet, Laura Coe Moore. His poems have appeared in* Spoon River Poetry Review, Columbia Journal, Cream City Review, Western Humanities Review *and others. His chapbook* Boys *is forthcoming from Duck Lake Books in February 2020. His first book,* Waxing the Dents, *was a finalist for the Brick Road Poetry Book Prize and will be released in April 2020.*

Joshua Lindenbaum's *poetry has appeared or is forthcoming in* Drunk Monkeys, West Texas Literary Review, HEArt Online, Breadcrumbs, Yes Poetry, The Bangalore Review, Five:2:One, 3Elements Review, Typishly *and several other publications. He's been workin' as an adjunct for seven years, and, although exploitation does not provide a warm-fuzzy feeling, he enjoys teaching. Currently, he's pursuing a PhD in English and creative writing at Binghamton University. The pen has been his companion for quite some time, but it's still waiting for him "to put a ring on it." It will even blast Beyoncé songs from time to time from a large boombox.*

Misty Cripps *is a former interaction designer and current dog- and parrot-lover living in Austin, Texas.*

San Antonian **Alex Z. Salinas** *earned a bachelor's degree in political science from St. Mary's University in 2011. His flash fiction has appeared online in* Every Day Fiction, Nanoism, escarp, 101 Words, 101 Fiction, *and* ZeroFlash. *He has also had poetry published in the* San Antonio Express-News. *He is the* San Antonio Review*'s poetry editor.*

William O. Pate II *is the publisher and editor of the* San Antonio Review. *He lives in Austin with his wife, four dogs and parrot and works in marketing. He has published* an examination of free will *at www.inadequate.net for over 20 years.*

Supporters | Thank you!

We greatly appreciate the financial support of the following donors:

- Deborah Marie Dera, *Runnemede, New Jersey*
- Stan Gunn, *Charlottesville, Virginia*
- Melody Klinger, *Austin, Texas*
- Barbara Elaine Leeper, *Austin, Texas*
- Mary Ellen & William Pate, *Leander, Texas*
- Mary Jo Pate, *Georgetown, Texas*
- Paul Peterson, *Austin, Texas*
- Teri Pitts, *Dover, New Hampshire*
- Rex Wilder, *Los Angeles, California*

Add your name to the above list by donating any amount.

Thank you!

The *San Antonio Review* is a costly endeavor undertaken with love by its editors and publisher. It is not a profit-seeking enterprise. It aims to herald interesting voices in the arts. It receives no financial support beyond donations and submission fees, which are used to recover some of the ongoing costs of web hosting, printing and other infrastructure.

www.sa-review.com

William Pate, *San Antonio Review*, P.O. Box 49589, Austin, Texas, 78765

www.ingramcontent.com/pod-product-compliance
Lightning Source LLC
Chambersburg PA
CBHW070438010526
44118CB00014B/2095